Frost Hollows and
Other Microclimates

Frost Hollows and Other Microclimates

By Laurence Pringle

William Morrow and Company
New York   1981

Printed in the United States of America.
1   2   3   4   5   6   7   8   9   10

Library of Congress Cataloging in Publication Data

Pringle, Laurence P.
  Frost hollows and other microclimates.

  Bibliography: p. 60
  Includes index.
  Summary: Discusses the variations of climates in small areas and how these microclimates affect plants, animals, agriculture, and architecture.
  1. Microclimatology—Juvenile literature. [1. Microclimatology. 2. Climatology] I. Title.
QC981.7.M5P74   551.6   81-4066
ISBN 0-688-00714-7   AACR2
ISBN 0-688-00715-5 (lib. bdg.)

Photo Credits

All photographs are by the author with the exception of the following: Bureau of Land Management, p. 44; National Park Service, Fred W. Mang, Jr., p. 43, M. Woodbridge Williams, p. 10; National Oceanic and Atmospheric Administration, p. 22; United Press International, p. 55; United States Department of Agriculture, Office of Governmental and Public Affairs, T. O. Driscoll, p. 53, Office of Information, A. Klinnert, p. 49; United States Weather Bureau, p. 21. Permission is gratefully acknowledged.

The author wishes to thank Verne N. Rockcastle,
Professor of Science and Environmental Education,
Cornell University,
for reading the manuscript of this book
and helping to improve its accuracy.

Contents

1/What Makes a Microclimate?

When you hear the word *climate*, you may think of Arctic ice and cold, or the dry, sunny warmth of the Southwest. You know that winds, the amount of rain or snow, the average temperature, and other weather conditions making up the year-round climate of a place vary from region to region.

Perhaps you have noticed that the climate also varies within the area where you live. Take temperature, for instance. One morning the official Weather Service temperature may be 32 degrees Fahrenheit (0 degrees Celsius). But the thermometer outside your window reads 29 degrees Fahrenheit (−1.7 degrees Celsius). And a

The overall climate of the Arctic is cold and dry.

Anywhere on land, whether in the Arctic or a desert,
you can find separate little climates close to the ground.

friend says that it is 24 degrees Fahrenheit (−4.4 degrees Celsius) where she lives. Within your own neigh-
borhood, there seem to be several little climates. In fact,
once you begin to investigate little climates, you may
find that the climate varies between one side of a house
and another, between one side of a tree and another,
and even between one side of a leaf and another.

11

Scientists have studied little climates, or microclimates, for many years. Their findings show that all life on land is tied inescapably to its surrounding microclimate. They also show that microclimates affect the quality and quantity of food crops and the amount of energy needed to heat or cool buildings—matters of vital importance to everyone on Earth.

A good example of a microclimate is an ocean beach in the summertime. On a sunny day, the land surface absorbs more heat energy from the sun than the ocean surface does. The land and the air above it become warmer. The air becomes lighter and rises. Cooler air over the ocean starts flowing to the area of lower air pressure. The result: a steady cool breeze blowing in from the sea.

Thanks to the special microclimate of the land-sea border, the seashore is often an ideal place to fly a kite.

At night, the flow of air at the shore usually reverses. The land cools quickly after sunset, because soil is a poor conductor of heat; only the top few inches are warmed very much.

Water loses its heat more slowly. Soon the ocean water and the air above it are somewhat warmer than the land. Air from the land flows toward the area of lower pressure, causing a land-to-sea breeze.

Seashore winds affect much more than kite flyers. Winds from the sea are moist with salty water vapor.

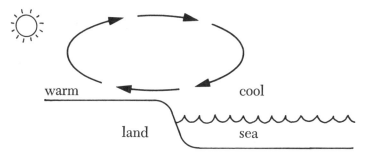

EARLY AFTERNOON SEA-TO-LAND BREEZE

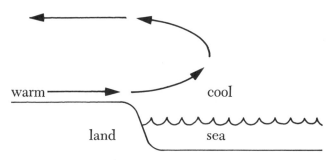

LATE EVENING LAND-TO-SEA BREEZE

Salt is deposited on soil and plants, with the heaviest salt concentrations close to shore.

On seaside dunes, you will find plants that thrive under salty, windy conditions. They are also able to withstand the high temperatures of the sunlit sand. Beach grass and salt-spray rose are two such plants. They are well-adapted to the special microclimate of the seashore dunes, an environment that is deadly for most other kinds of plants.

The winds of a seashore microclimate are the result of some basic physical facts of nature: different surfaces warm or cool at different rates, warmed air gets lighter,

13

cooler air pushes it upward. Such factors help create all climates—big and little. Let's see what other factors help make microclimates, then explore their effects on living things.

The sun's radiant energy is the driving force behind the earth's winds, the ocean's currents, and the water cycle of the atmosphere. As the example of the sea breezes shows, some surfaces absorb solar energy more quickly than others. In general, dark surfaces soak up more radiant energy than light-colored ones. On a hot summer day, if you want to test the old saying about the weather being "hot enough to fry an egg on the sidewalk," choose the darkest sidewalk you can find.

Dark soils and dark roofs also absorb more sun energy than light ones. And clean snow absorbs very little. It reflects away at least three-quarters of the solar energy that falls on it.

After a snowfall, you can sometimes see clear signs of how light and dark surfaces absorb different amounts of solar energy. On a cold but sunny afternoon, notice where the snow melts first. You will probably find melted holes and the first patches of bare earth around dark rocks, stems of plants, or other dark objects that stick out of the snow. The rocks may not be warm to the

Snow melts away from dark rocks,
because they absorb more solar energy than clean snow.

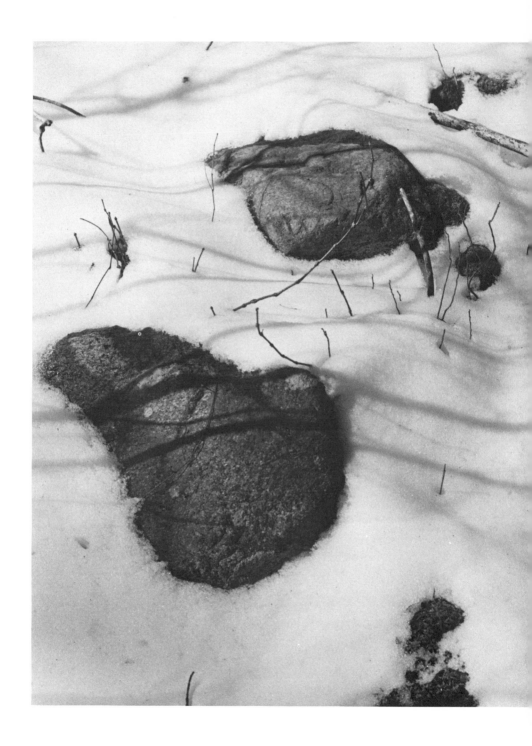

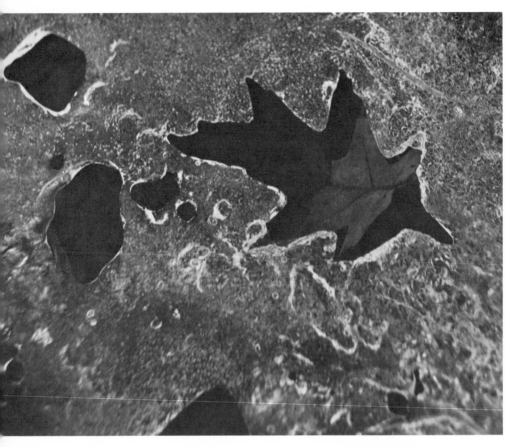

An oak leaf, frozen in the ice on a creek, absorbed enough
solar energy to melt the ice in the leaf's characteristic shape.

touch, but they absorb much more solar energy than the
surrounding snow does.

Sunlight does not always warm a dark surface more
than a light-colored one. As you walk along a beach, you
will find that dry sand is hotter to step on than wet sand,
even though the dry sand is lighter in color. Wet sand

16

A beach is a good place to explore microclimates.

does absorb more radiant energy, but some of the energy is given off as water evaporates from the sand. Some heat is also conducted down into wet sand. Dry sand is a poor heat conductor.

Water warms more thoroughly than land does, as solar radiation penetrates deeply and currents mix and move the water. Once a lake or ocean warms up during the summer, it retains the heat well into the fall and winter. The heat radiates to the atmosphere gradually, and so coastal dwellers experience milder winters than people living farther inland.

As you can see, the climate of different places can vary a lot, just by taking different colors, surfaces, and substances into account. When you add the factors of topography (the shape of the land) and of plant life, the variety of little climates seems endless.

The shape of the land affects the amount of sunlight it receives. People who live just east of big hills, mountains, or even tall buildings know this phenomenon. For them, "sunset" may occur at three o'clock in the afternoon.

The angle of the sunlight reaching Earth's surface changes through the year, which also affects the amount of sunlight a slope receives. (This difference is most important in the temperate regions, not in the tropics where the angle of the sunlight striking the surface does not vary as much during the year.) In the northern hemi-

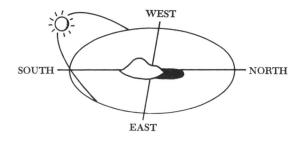

Winter solstice, December 21

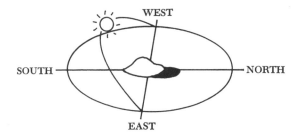

Spring and autumn equinoxes, March 21 and September 21

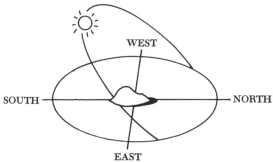

Summer solstice, June 21

As the Earth travels once around the sun each year,
the north pole tilts toward the sun in summer
and away from the sun in winter (in the northern hemisphere).
As a result the sun's path across the sky
is lowest in winter and highest in summer.

19

sphere, north-facing slopes receive less sunlight than hillsides facing in other directions. South-facing slopes receive the greatest amount of sunlight. So north-facing or south-facing slopes within the same valley have entirely different climates.

The shape of the land also affects the flow of air. When air close to the land cools at night, it becomes dense and tends to flow downhill. The air movement is called a gravity wind by meteorologists (scientists who study weather). Cool air acts like a fluid. It collects in valleys and hollows, and it cools further as heat radiates into the atmosphere. Depending on the season, the cool air may cause fog or frost to form.

Little valleys and basins where cold air settles are called "frost hollows." The world's most famous frost hollow is located on a plateau in the Austrian Alps. The Gstettneralm frost hollow is about 500 feet (150 meters) deep. One March night the temperature at the top of the hollow was 0 degrees Fahrenheit (−18 degrees Celsius), while the temperature at the bottom was −49 degrees Fahrenheit (−31 degrees Celsius). In frost hollows, freezing temperatures can occur in midsummer.

Air movement is influenced by plants as well. You may have noticed how a strong wind loses its force in a forest. It is slowed by friction between the moving air and the tree trunks, branches, and leaves. Even grass on a lawn exerts a drag on wind. So does a bare soil surface. A ten-

A valley may fill with fog when cool air collects in it overnight.

mile-an-hour wind at a height of six and a half feet (two meters) may slow to one mile an hour, or less, close to the ground.

Plants affect all of the factors that make up microclimates. By casting shade and by giving off water vapor, plants make the air around them cooler and more humid.

Weather-recording instruments are usually kept several feet above ground, to avoid the effects of microclimates.

Good examples are the dark, humid, still microclimates underfoot in the grassy jungles of meadows and lawns.

When you think of the ways in which climate can be influenced by plants, topography, surface color, and other factors, you can understand why meteorologists place their weather-recording instruments up off the ground. Instruments used to measure temperature and relative humidity are kept in shelters at least five feet (one and a half meters) above the surface, out in the open. Conditions there are more moderate and stable than they are close to the ground. In this way, meteorologists gather data on the general regional weather and avoid most of the effects of microclimates.

"The climate near the ground" is one definition of microclimate. However it is defined, microclimate is the real climate that affects every plant and animal on the land.

The greatest effects of microclimates exist at or near the ground, where many plants and animals live.

2/Plants and Animals

If you put a shade-"loving" houseplant by a sunny window, it will soon be in trouble and may die. Rooted and immobile, plants cannot flee from a hostile environment. Both houseplants and outdoor plants live in special microclimates. Different parts of plants often have different microclimates. And plants also affect the little climates of neighboring plants and of animals.

Forests are good places to observe some of these effects. Treetops receive a maximum amount of sunlight and strong, turbulent winds. Below, the microclimate of the forest floor is usually a dramatically different world. In a dense evergreen forest, only about 10 percent of the available sunlight reaches the floor. The temperature there may be 20 to 30 degrees Fahrenheit (10 to 15 degrees Celsius) cooler than the temperature of bare soil in a field.

In deciduous forests, however, the microclimates vary more as the seasons change. Solar rays are not hindered much during the winter and early spring. Dead leaves on the forest floor are poor conductors of heat, so their temperature may soar to 109 degrees Fahrenheit (43 degrees Celsius) on sunny spring days. Many woodland wild flowers sprout, bloom, and make and store food during this brief time of intense sunlight. This is a difficult period for shrews, snails, and other animals that cannot tolerate high temperatures and low humidity. Before long, however, their favored cool, humid microclimate is created as tree leaves open and block the sunlight.

Whether they grow alone or in groups, trees, shrubs, and other plants affect the microclimate beneath and near them. On a frosty autumn morning you may find a frost-free circle under a tree. It exists because the tree's branches and leaves slowed the radiation of heat from the soil, so that the patch of ground was warmer than the surrounding land.

Trees also affect the amount and the distribution of rain and snow reaching the ground. Under a tree any precipitation takes more time to hit the earth; the leafy crown must get wet before water drips through. Trees with

The leaves of many woodland wild flowers absorb much solar energy before the leaves of trees overhead open.

26

Land snails thrive in the cool, moist forest floor microclimate.

smooth bark have large flows of rainwater down their trunks. Measurements show that up to half of the rain caught by the leaves of beech trees runs along twigs, limbs, and finally down the trunk. For many kinds of rough-barked trees and especially for evergreens, however, the greatest concentration of rainwater drips to the ground from the outer edges of the tree's crown. The same is true of snow. It is often deepest just under the outer edges of a tree's crown.

A tree affects the amount and the distribution of snow or rain
that reaches the ground beneath it.

Wet snow may cling to branches for days. Some of it
evaporates there and never reaches the ground. The rest
eventually crashes down during a thaw or a high wind.
Somewhat protected from the sun, snow under trees
melts more slowly than snow in the open. In the spring,

Why did snow remain on the north side of this tree?

you may find patches of snow under evergreens long after it has melted elsewhere. (Early spring is often a good time to observe the effects of microclimates. Try to figure out why snow remains in some places and not in others.)

Trees and forests protect the plants and animals living at ground level, as they are not faced with the climatic extremes of more open spaces. Even in the treeless Arctic, however, plants are adapted in ways that reduce the extremes of the climate around them. They grow close to the ground, out of the cold, drying winds. The leaves and stems of many plants are densely covered with "hairs," which help form an insulating layer of still air at the plant's outer surface. They also help prevent water loss from the tiny pores on leaves and stems.

Arctic flowers need warmth in order to develop and to produce seeds in a summer that lasts only four to six weeks. Some flowers are bell-shaped. Hanging down, they trap heat that rises from the ground. Arctic poppy flowers turn and follow the sun across the sky. The petals are shaped in a way that allows the sun's heat to concentrate on the center, where seeds develop. In such ways, Arctic flowers have special little climates that enable them to reproduce.

Desert plants also have ways to moderate a harsh climate. Cactus spines cast cooling shade on the plant surface. Like the "hairs" on Arctic plants, the spines too slow the force of the wind. As a result, the outer surfaces of a cactus plant are exposed to a microclimate that is

Spines affect the microclimate at the surface of a cactus plant.

cooler and calmer than the climate of the surrounding air. At the hottest, driest time of the year, some desert plants are able to turn their leaves so that only the narrow edges face the direct rays of the sun. The microclimate surrounding each leaf is cooled and its loss of water reduced.

The most extreme temperature ranges on Earth have been recorded on bare desert soils—as high as 150 degrees Fahrenheit (66 degrees Celsius) by day, then sharply cooler, as low as 60 degrees Fahrenheit (16 degrees Celsius) by night. The air is very dry. Yet about forty inches (one meter) underground the temperature is moderate and stays the same day after day. No wonder that many rodents and reptiles prefer to live in the microclimate of underground burrows.

Nonburrowing animals, such as jackrabbits, seek shady places or little hollows that have cooler temperatures than open spaces. A coyote may dig a little depression to lie in. You may have seen a pet dog do the same on a hot summer day. Since soil conducts heat poorly, the temperature just a short distance underground is bound to be much cooler than the surface.

A German scientist visiting the southwestern United States noticed the effects of microclimate on the giant saguaro cactus. He discovered that flowers bloomed first on the cactus's southwest side and not at all on the northeast side. In other regions, similar observations have

A coyote is cooled in a microclimate created by shade.

been made of fruit trees and pine trees. In temperate regions of the northern hemisphere, the southwestern side
of virtually any object or slope receives more solar radiation than other sides.

You can see dramatic evidence of this fact in parts of
the Rocky Mountains. South-facing slopes are more sun-

lit, warm, and dry than north-facing slopes. They are sparsely covered with juniper, ponderosa pine, and grasses. The moist, cool, north-facing slopes are densely covered with spruce, fir, and grasses.

You can see similar effects in forests in many parts of the United States. In some regions, evergreens grow on north-facing slopes and deciduous trees on south-facing slopes. The exposure of different slopes affects the distribution and abundance of shrubs, ferns, mosses, and wild flowers, too. In Wisconsin, meteorologists found that the frost-free growing season was 153 days on slopes that faced the southwest and 147 days on those that faced northeast.

These differences in the amount of solar radiation received have many small-scale effects as well. If you travel in the wintertime along a road that runs east and west, compare the amount of snow on the hillsides near the road. Usually the snow on the south-facing slope melts before the snow on the opposite side. Deer and elk know this pattern. In the early spring, when the snow may still be deep in the woods and especially on north-facing slopes, they gather in great numbers on open south-facing slopes. There the snow melts first, so travel and foraging are easier.

Snow remains on the opposite slope, which faces north, and not on the south-facing slope in the foreground.

A white-tailed deer in Minnesota runs easily
along a south-facing riverbank where snow has melted.

36

Ants move masses of eggs to microclimates
that are suitable for their development.

Small animals are also affected by similar microclimates. Like a mountain, a dome-shaped anthill receives varying amounts of sunlight on its different sides. Depending on the season, ants living inside may concentrate their activities and store their eggs on the cooler north side or the warmer south side. In Oregon, a biolo-

37

On cold days, pigeons bask in the warmth of the morning sun on the east side of buildings.

gist saw carpenter ants emerging in the spring from holes in the south side of fir trees, even though the surrounding snow was still six feet deep.

"Moss always grows on the north side of trees" is an old saying. This woods lore is supposed to be used by people who are lost, to help them establish their direction. A tree trunk does receive the least amount of solar radiation on its north side, which may help create a cool, moist microclimate for mosses and algae. In fact, the "moss" that we see on tree trunks, stones, and other objects is usually an alga named *Pleurococcus*. Sometimes, however, you can find this alga growing on all sides of a tree trunk. And, since *Pleurococcus* thrives in a humid

An alga grows most abundantly on the north side of this tree, but it does not always do so.

microclimate, you might find it growing abundantly on the *south* side of a tree, when that side faces a nearby lake or stream. Since a microclimate may be the result of several factors, growth of algae or mosses on a tree is no foolproof guide to north.

Plant growth can be affected by tiny changes in the land surface. Norwegian scientists discovered that long-lasting hoofprints of reindeer and footprints of people became places where a certain kind of moss flourished. The moss was rarely found elsewhere. In some unknown way, the footprint microclimates were different enough from those of the surroundings to make its growth possible.

You don't have to visit faraway places in order to see examples of microclimates. You can observe and investigate their effects near your home. Notice the flowers that appear on a shrub or tree that stands out in the open. Do they all blossom at the same time? If not, use a compass to figure out on which side they open first and last. Also compare the flowering times of plants on the north side of a building with those on the south side.

A rock or board lying on the ground is often a good place to see how little climates affect the lives of small animals. On a clear, sunny day the object and the soil surrounding it may seem like a sunbaked desert. Press the tip of a thermometer right against the object to find its temperature. (The kind of fast-responding thermom-

Sow bugs, slugs, and many other small animals
thrive in cool, moist microclimates under rocks.

eter used in photographic darkrooms is good for this in-
vestigation.)

Then lift the rock or board. Underneath you may find
ants, sow bugs, crickets, a salamander, or other animals
that cannot survive for long in a hot, dry climate. Compare the temperature under the rock with the temperature on its top.

Little climates are all around us, on distant mountain
slopes and underfoot.

3/Architecture and Agriculture

People have been aware of microclimates for a long time. About 320 B.C., the Greek naturalist Theophrastus wrote about "hollow places" being "chilled by winds arising locally." Much earlier, knowledge about microclimates was used in agriculture and in the design, color, and materials used in clothing and buildings.

In the southwestern United States, certain Indian dwellings (such as Mesa Verde in Colorado) were built in the sides of cliffs so they were naturally protected from full summer sunlight, which comes from high in the sky. In the winter, however, they received maximum available sunlight as the angle of the sun's rays was

42

lower and struck the sides of the cliff more than the top. Also in the Southwest, the thick walls of adobe buildings absorb heat slowly during the day. They radiate the heat slowly at night. Thus, the temperature indoors does not change nearly as much as outdoors.

Cliff dwellings at Mesa Verde National Park in Colorado.

Indian cliff dwellings are warmed by the low sun of wintertime.

Eskimo igloos are designed to shut out cold and wind. An igloo's entrance is low and faces away from prevailing winds. Snow is piled around the ice-block structure to provide insulation. The temperature inside the igloo is raised by oil lamps and by body heat. It may be 65 degrees Fahrenheit (36 degrees Celsius) above the outdoor temperature.

The saltbox house, designed for New England winters, has a long sloping roof that faces north. This design reduces the chilling effect of winds from that direction. Closer to the equator, in the Mediterranean and Middle

44

Eastern regions, living spaces are usually open to the north, to take advantage of the cooling effects of that exposure.

Sometimes people forget or ignore the effects of microclimates on buildings and suffer the consequences. Until the early 1970s, when an era of cheap energy ended, large skyscrapers built in the United States seemed designed to waste energy. The materials used, especially single panes of glass, allowed great indoor heat gain in summer and great heat loss in winter. Thus, the costs of heating and cooling were raised tremendously. Frequently windows could not be opened to

Both the Eskimo igloo and the New England saltbox house were designed to fend off wind and cold from the north.

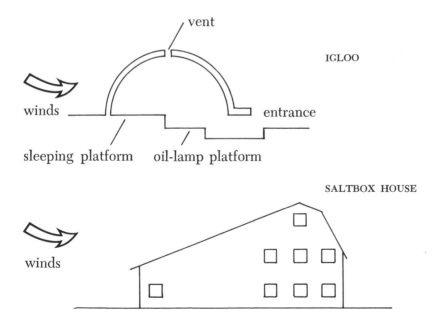

take advantage of comfortable outdoor air when it was present, which added further to costs. One well-known architect admitted that only massive air conditioning made his glass buildings tolerable places in which to work. Similar mistakes were made in the construction of single family homes, too.

Rising energy costs are bringing an end to this waste. Architects are rediscovering ways to take advantage of microclimates and their effects. For example, placing a house so that the sides with the most surface area face north and south, not east and west, is advantageous. This location reduces excessive heat gain in the summer as the maximum sunlight hits the house on the west side. Having few windows on the north-facing side reduces heat loss in winter.

On the other hand, large south-facing windows can capture heat from the winter sun. Overhanging roofs, shades, or other devices keep them from admitting excessive heat in the summer. In fact, there are several ways to store the heat and circulate it to warm the rest of the building and to provide hot water. A comfortable microclimate for people can be created without using great amounts of fuel for cooling or heating.

Trees and shrubs planted near a house can influence its surrounding microclimate. On the south and west side, deciduous trees shade the roof and walls in the summertime. After their leaves fall, winter sunlight can

46

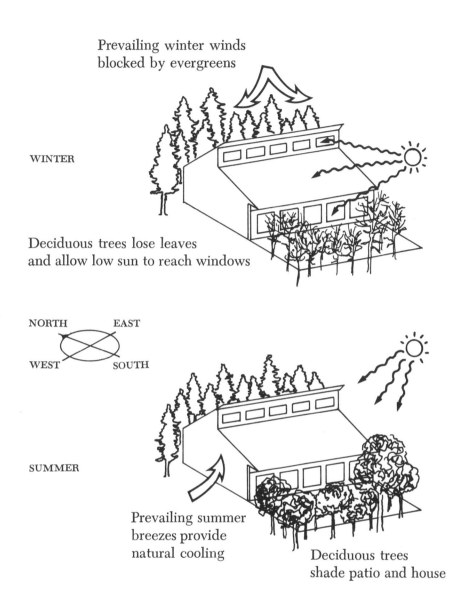

Prevailing winter winds
blocked by evergreens

WINTER

Deciduous trees lose leaves
and allow low sun to reach windows

NORTH   EAST

WEST   SOUTH

SUMMER

Prevailing summer
breezes provide
natural cooling

Deciduous trees
shade patio and house

A building's position on the land and the plants around it
can greatly affect its microclimate, energy costs,
and the comfort of the people who live in it.

47

more easily warm and light the house. Evergreens on the northern side slow winter winds and help insulate the house from the cold.

Trees are sometimes planted to affect the microclimates of croplands. During a severe drought in the 1930s, wind erosion turned parts of the Great Plains into a dust bowl. To conserve the remaining soil, long rows of trees called "windbreaks" or "shelterbelts" were planted across the direction of prevailing winds. Shelterbelts are often four or five rows deep. The goal was simple: to slow the winds and thereby reduce loss of soil. Research shows that shelterbelts do so. Other benefits have been discovered, however, as scientists made observations and even used wind tunnels to test models of different kinds of windbreaks.

Slowing the wind reduces the evaporation of soil moisture. Windbreaks also cause wind-driven snow to accumulate in the fields they shelter. The melting snow adds water to the soil. Overall, shelterbelts change the microclimate enough so that yields of wheat and other crops increase in the sheltered areas.

Investigators have found, too, that gaps in shelterbelts create a sort of funnel. Wind speed increases through gaps. These jets of wind may damage crops and lessen the beneficial effects of the little climates created by the shelterbelts.

Sometimes a row of trees, a stone wall, or other wind-

This shelterbelt caused ten-foot-high drifts of snow
to pile up at the edge of a farmer's field.

breaks can have a damaging effect on crops. The obstacle
may block the flow of cool air downhill in an orchard,
for instance. It dams the air, causing a cool air lake to
form. The result may be poor growth or frost damage
in the lowest part of the orchard. A cold air dam is some-
thing like a frost hollow.

Most fruit growers know enough about microclimates
to avoid planting trees in frost hollows or places where
cold air is dammed. They also try to influence microclimates by preventing much growth of vegetation under

49

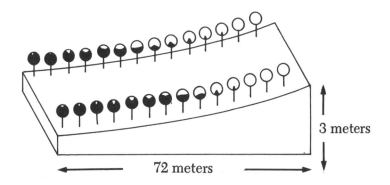

3 meters

72 meters

This drawing shows the effects of a cold-air dam on a peach orchard.
The black area on trees indicates where peach fruit was frozen.
The light areas, above the "lake" of coldest air, escaped damage.

their trees. In this way heat can radiate more readily
from the soil at night—sometimes an aid in preventing
frost damage.

Knowledge about little climates is vital to anyone who
tries to grow wine grapes. Small differences in climate
affect the survival, development, and flavor of different
grape varieties. In recent years, careful study of microclimates led to the establishment of vineyards in Oregon,
Washington, Idaho, Michigan, Virginia, and on Long
Island in New York State.

Vineyards, especially in regions having colder climates, are usually planted on south-facing hillsides. A
southern exposure gives the grape plants a dry, sunny
microclimate and protection from early autumn and late
spring frosts. Lake hillsides are favored places. Lake

50

water warms the valley air and helps prevent damage to grape vines during the cold seasons. Sunlight reflected from lakes to hillsides is beneficial to vineyards too.

Many vineyards are divided by stone walls, which reflect sunlight onto the vines and also radiate heat at night. The walls generally extend up and down slopes, so that they slow crosswinds and channel the flow of cold air downhill. Vineyard microclimates are also affected by such factors as the spaces between rows of plants and the direction of the rows. Small differences in temperature can be crucial. They can minimize the risk of fungus diseases and enhance the flavor of wine made from the grapes.

In some far northern vineyards, vines of highly valued European grape varieties are grafted onto the stalks of native vines at a point three to four feet above the ground. In this way, the hardy native stalks endure the coldest temperatures while the more tender varieties have a milder microclimate in which to bear fruit.

Microclimates affect all agriculture, from forests to home gardens. Agricultural scientists continue to study the effects of little climates on plants and of plants on little climates.

Research shows that the amount of space left between individual plants or between rows of plants greatly affects wind speed, soil temperature, and the amount of moisture in the soil and air. A dense crop, such as alfalfa, keeps the soil surface dark, cool, and calm. The field of a more open crop, such as corn, is sunnier, warmer, and windier, so the soil surface is warmer and drier. These differences affect plant growth and the populations of pests and animals that prey on the plants. In some cases, farmers adjust their harvesting schedule or methods according to these differences in order to reduce the numbers of pests or increase the numbers of the natural enemies of pests.

Ladybird beetles are natural enemies of aphids.

Hot caps provide a warm microclimate
around frost-sensitive garden plants.

Farmers and gardeners have used knowledge of microclimates for many years. When a spring frost threatens
young squash or melon plants, for example, gardeners
cover the plants in the late afternoon. Sometimes hot
caps, shaped like hats, are used. The caps trap warm air
radiating from the soil, then are removed in the morning
when the danger of frost is over.

A covering of dead leaves or straw, called a "mulch," also protects young plants from frost. Mostly, however, mulches are left on the ground throughout the growing season. They block the evaporation of soil moisture and help ensure a steady supply of water for crops. On the other hand, mulches may provide shelter and a favorable microclimate for some crop pests. Sometimes a farmer can help solve pest problems by turning over the cozy mulch in the wintertime, exposing the insects to freezing temperatures.

Agriculture and architecture are just two activities in which the influences of microclimates are commonly used. You can be sure that people choosing a site for a ski resort first study the microclimate of different mountain slopes. When airport planners lay out the position and direction of runways, they consider wind speed and direction, fog, and other local climate conditions. To some extent, of course, building the airport changes these conditions for better or worse.

Highway engineers must also deal with such problems as fog, ice, and drifting snow. In the autumn, fences of wooden slats are placed in fields on the windward side of roads. Like shelterbelts, these snow fences, or drift fences, cause the wind-driven snow to settle in fields rather than on the highways.

Some road problems have no easy solution, except to alert motorists to possible hazards. You may have seen

On some highways, microclimates cause sudden changes
from clear to foggy conditions, with disastrous results.

and wondered about signs that warn: *Bridge Freezes
Before Highway.* The temperature of the road surface
is affected by what lies underneath. Rocks and soil give
up some heat to the road. Only air lies directly under a
bridge, however, so the bridge surface cools faster than
the road surface.

Once you begin to think about little climates and what
makes one different from another, you may start to find
them everywhere about you. A house or apartment has
many little climates.

There are places where houseplants die and places

where they thrive. Without meaning to, people give cockroaches the microclimate they prefer. Tropical insects, they find the warmth and moisture available in kitchens and bathrooms beneficial. The fungi known as mildew need warmth and humidity to grow, and they appear on walls and other objects where these conditions are provided.

Like other animals, humans need a certain climate surrounding their body in order to live and be comfortable. Clothes, heating, and air conditioning are ways people keep the temperature and humidity to their liking. Astronauts in space carry an Earth microclimate inside their space suit.

With or without clothes, however, even the human body has a range of little climates. A *Scientific American* article titled "Life on the Human Skin" referred to "the desert of the forearm, the cool woods of the scalp, and the tropical forest of the armpit." The differences between little climates on the human body are small but measurable.

Consider the fungi called *Tinea pedis*, which normally lives between human toes and is not noticed. Occasionally it multiplies and becomes an itching, irritating infection. It is called "athlete's foot." No one ever has to worry about an outbreak of "athlete's elbow" or "athlete's earlobe" because *Tinea pedis* needs the special humid microclimate it finds between the toes.

56

Learning about microclimates can be fun. And whether you want to save energy, fly a kite, grow plants, or keep cool on a hot summer day, knowledge of the little climates that surround you will be helpful.

A house cat basks in the warmth of spring sunshine.

Glossary

atmosphere—the whole mass of gases that surrounds Earth (or any planet).

climate—the average long-term atmospheric conditions, including temperature, precipitation, and wind, that prevail in a particular place.

deciduous—refers to broad-leaved plants that drop their leaves at the end of each growing season.

environment—all of the surroundings of an organism, including other living things, climate, and soils.

evaporation—the process by which a liquid is changed to a vapor (gas). Every gram of water converted to vapor requires about 580 calories of energy.

evergreens—plants that retain their leaves for more than one growing season.

fungi—a group of plants lacking roots, stems, leaves, and the green coloring substance chlorophyll. Fungi includes yeasts, molds, and mushrooms.

humidity—the amount of water vapor in the air at a given temperature compared to the amount it can hold. Humidity is relative, since the amount of water a parcel of air can contain depends on its temperature and pressure. When it contains the maximum amount we say the relative humidity is 100 percent. Dry regions normally have relative humidities of 10 to 30 percent.

meteorology—the study of the atmosphere, especially the weather. The study of climate is known as climatology.

microclimate—the climate in the immediate vicinity of an object or organism. It is the climate that is really significant for the comfort and survival of an organism.

radiant energy—energy transferred in the form of visible light rays and also invisible ultraviolet, infrared, and X rays. Most radiation from the sun is in the form of visible light. Once absorbed, radiant energy is converted to heat energy.

temperate—having a mild climate, neither tropical nor polar.

topography—the shape of the land surface, including the position of lakes, streams, and other features.

water cycle—the ceaseless cycle of water condensing from the atmosphere and falling to Earth's surface, then evaporating into the atmosphere. In a year, 580 trillion tons of water are exchanged between Earth and its atmosphere.

weather—the general atmospheric conditions, including winds, precipitation, humidity, and temperature, that exist at any given time and place.

Further Reading

Gates, David, *Man and His Environment: Climate.* New York: Harper & Row, 1972.

Geiger, Rudolf, *The Climate Near the Ground.* Cambridge, Mass.: Harvard University Press, 1965.

Griffiths, John, *Applied Climatology: An Introduction.* New York: Oxford University Press, 1966.

Griffiths, John, *Climate and the Environment.* Boulder, Colorado: Westview Press, 1976.

Marples, Mary, "Life on the Human Skin." *Scientific American,* January 1969, pp. 108-115.

Rockcastle, Verne, *Little Climates.* Ithaca, New York: Cornell Science Leaflets, 1961 (out of print).

Rosenberg, Norman, *Microclimate: The Biological Environment.* New York: John Wiley & Sons, 1974.

Watts, May Theilgaard, *Reading the Landscape in America.* New York: Macmillan Publishing Company, 1975.

Index

61

ABOUT THE AUTHOR

Born in Rochester, N.Y., Laurence Pringle attended Cornell University, where he graduated with a B.S. in wildlife conservation. Later, at the University of Massachusetts, he earned an M.S. on the same subject, and he also studied journalism at Syracuse University. Upon finishing his studies, Mr. Pringle taught high-school science for one year and for seven years was an editor of *Nature and Science*, a children's magazine published at the American Museum of Natural History in New York City. Since 1970 he has been a free-lance writer, photographer, and editor. He has three teen-age children and lives in West Nyack, New York.

DISCARD